Frog Opera,

WITH

Pollywog Chorus.

A Musical Extravaganza

FOUNDED UPON THE NURSERY TALE AND OLD SONG OF

"A FROG HE WOULD A WOOING GO."

PROVIDENCE:
PRESS OF J. A. & R. A. REID.
1880.

All communications concerning the production of the FROG OPERA, should be addressed,

STUART ROGERS,

PROVIDENCE, R. I.

CHARACTERS REPRESENTED.

PRINCE FROG. ROBBER KITTEN. BARONESS RAT.
SIMON (his Squire). GYPSY CHIEF. MISS MOUSE.
BARON RAT. FROG SENTINEL. CHILD FROG.
SIR THOMAS CAT. QUEEN FROG. FOUR BRAVE FROGS.
Chorus of Pollywogs, Gypsies, Rats and Mice.

Incidental Music.

ACT I—Banks of the Danube.

1. Opening Chorus, "Simon says Up" .... Chorus.
2. Chorus, "Beautiful Tails" .... Pollywogs.
3. Song, "For thy dear Sake" .... Prince Frog.
4. Song, "True as Steel" .... Simon.
5. Quartette, "The Bullfrog" .... Prince Frog's Retainers.
6. Duet, "What can the Matter be" .... Queen and Child.
7. Song and Chorus .... Prince and Chorus.
8. Grand Finale .... Prince, Simon and Chorus.

ACT II—The Gypsy Camp.

9. Gypsy Chorus and Dance .... Gypsies.
10. Trio, "These are Gypsies" .... Prince, Simon and Baron.
11. Chorus, "To-night, To-night," .... Gypsies.
12. Song and Chorus, "Life of a Gypsy" .... Gypsy Chief and Chorus.
13. Duet, "Seeking Grandeur" .... Baroness, Rat and Prince.
14. Duet, "Hey Diddle, Diddle" .... Sir Thomas Cat and Robber Kitten.
15. Song and Chorus .... Simon and Frogs.
16. Chorus, "Oh! Mother Dear" .... Pollywogs.
17. Aria, "Too Late" .... Queen Frog.
18. Recitative, Duet and Finale .... The Cats.

ACT III—The Old Mill.

19. Serenade and Duet, "Star of my Night" .... Prince, Miss Mouse and Chorus.
20. Duet, "O Aunty Dear" .... Baroness and Miss Mouse.
21. "Call it not Fancy" .... Baron Rat.
22. Aria, "Not this Wedding" .... Baroness Rat.
23. Duet, "Mournful Ditty" .... Thomas Cat and Kitten.
24. Quarreling Duet, "More Rows" .... Thomas Cat and Kitten.
25. Song, "Pollywoggy Paradise" .... Simon.
26. Chorus and March, "Heigho! said Rowley" .... Wedding Guests.
27. Drinking Song, "Let the Old Mill Ring" .... Chorus.
28. Song, "Spinning and Singing" .... Miss Mouse.
29. Grand Finale, "Oh! he will Win" .... Principals and Chorus.

ARGUMENT.

" There was a frog lived in a well,
  And a merry mouse lived in a mill.

This frog would a wooing go,
But could not walk for the corn on his toe ;
So he mounted and away did ride,
With a sword and pistol by his side.
He rode till he came to Miss Mouse's hall,
And then he did both knock and call,—
' Pray, Miss Mouse, are you within ?'
' O yes, kind sir, and going to spin.'
' Pray, Miss Mouse, will you marriage make
With a young frog that's tall and straight?'
' My Uncle Rat went out this morn,
And I won't consent till his return.'
Her Uncle Rat he did come home,
Saying, ' Who's been here since I've been gone?'
' There's been a noble, tall, straight man,
Who vows he'll marry me, if he can.'
' We'll have the wedding in the mill.'
' O, yes, kind Uncle, so we will.'
Now while they all at dinner sat,
In came the kitten and the cat.
The cat seized Uncle Rat by the crown,
The kitten pulled the poor wife down.
The mouse she did run up the wall,
And said, ' O, dear, they'll kill us all !'
The frog he did run up the brook,
And there he met a hungry duck.
The duck he swallowed him down his throat,
Saying, ' There's an end of these fine folk.' "

NURSERY TALES.

" A frog he would a wooing go,
Whether his mother would let him or no.
Off he set with his opera hat ;
On the road he met with a rat.
They soon arrived at Mouse's Hall ;
They gave a loud tap and they gave a loud call,—
' Pray, Mrs. Mouse, are you within ?'
' Yes, kind sirs, I'm sitting to spin.'
' Come, Mrs. Mouse, now give us some beer,
That Froggy and I may have some cheer.'
' Pray, Mr. Frog, will you give us a song?
Let the subject be something that's not very long.'
' Indeed, Mrs. Mouse,' replied the frog ;
' A cold has made me as hoarse as a hog.'
' Since you have caught cold, Mr. Frog,' Mousy said,
' I'll sing you a song that I have just made.'
As they were in glee and a merry making,
A cat and her kittens came tumbling in.
The cat she seized the rat by the crown ;
The kittens they pulled the little mouse down.
This put Mr. Frog in a terrible fright ;
He took up his hat and wished them good-night.
As Froggy was crossing it over a brook,
A lily-white duck came and gobbled him up.
So here is an end of one, two, three,—
The Rat, the Mouse, and little Froggy." "

OLD SONG.

Frog Opera

WITH

Pollywog Chorus.

ACT FIRST.— Banks of the Danube.

Scene First.— It is early dawn; the frogs and pollywogs, bold retainers of Queen Frog and her son, the Prince, are discovered reposing in the ancestral puddle, near a well, the home of a widowed Mother Frog and her boy — her first-born.

As morning breaks, the crowing of cocks is heard and answered, until soon the frog sentinel, who holds the morning watch, catches the sound, and in the same musical strain, croaks forth the glad tidings that he has news from Simon, a wayward, curious frog, who has ventured to visit the outer world, to gather news of fashions and gossip generally. The news received is, that "wigwag" is the style. The pollys are in high glee as they wake and discover that their tails are all in fashion. The pleasures of a pollywog are limited; the historian could conceive no greater and more suitable pastime for them than that of admiring the graceful swinging of their tails, although the presence of the newly acquired hands and feet show that the caudal appendage will soon be cast off, and all the youthful energies must be devoted to the new method of locomotion. The Prince, their brother, who now appears from the well, reminds them of this, and tells them to bid them good-bye.

> *Chorus.*— Beautiful tails, O beautiful tails,
>   Thy gentle wigwag is joyous and queer;
> How to our hearts thy switchery tells
>   Tails of the past ever dear.
> Wilt thou return once more to repeat
>   The thrill of our childhood and innocent play?
> Ah! must we say farewell to the fleet
>   And ravishing sweetness of day?
> Beautiful tails, O beautiful tails!
>   Thy gentle wigwag is joyous and queer;
> How to our hearts thy switchery tells
>   Tails of the past ever dear.

The Prince seems melancholy and thoughtful, and they leave him to himself, to brood over his wrongs, real or imaginary. 'Tis now that the spirit of insubordination seizes him, and he resolves that he " Will a wooing go, whether his mother will let him or no," and sings of his love and devotion for Miss Mouse. Before leaving home he looks about for some comrades, some squire and retinue, to share with him the toils and hardships of the tour he plans. He sees Simon just returning from his visit to the outside world. He chooses him as his body-guard. Simon is delighted and swears eternal loyalty and homage, and that he will be true as steel.

Song.—SIMON.

I will be true and staunch as steel,
   Tho' the fiends of a phœnix flare;
I will be true and staunch as steel,
   I will blight all their blazoned glare.
This strong right arm shall wield its fanchion flight
For thee alone, with all its quivering might.
   I'll be true as steel,
   Though thunder bolts burst on the sooty night.
   I'll be true as steel,
   Yet I will be true and staunch as steel.

I will be true and staunch as steel,
   I will stand 'twixt thee and death,
In either brook, or miry lea,
   I will fight with lingering breath.
Though 'round my head the slaughterous battle din,
I'll wade in gore up to my very chin,
To save my Prince, to bravely save our future king.
   I'll be true as steel,
   Yet I'll be true and staunch as steel,
   I'll be true, I'll be true, I'll be true and staunch to thee as steel

'T is now the rising hour of the Queen, and she appears from the well, and her courtiers, the pollywogs, follow her. The sulkiness of her son at once attracts her attention, and she extorts from him his secret. Now appears upon the scene one of those unaccountable phases of human nature: boys stoning bull-frogs, because all boys like to. These frogs were not exempt, and so they caught it; and amid this shower of assorted missiles, the figures of the Queen mother and her child frog stand out in bold relief, while they sing what they think is their own requiem, as follows:—

O, ma, what can the matter be?
Boys throwing stones, and trying to spatter ye.
But, ma, that stone would flatten me —
No, child, it's only a scare.
   They'll splash you and dash you,
   Take sticks and play thrash you;

They think 'tis their duty
  To try and make hash of you.
'Tis only their fun, child,
  But may be the death of you.
Law, child, why, I wouldn't care.

QUEEN FROG AND CHILD.

O, ma, your trying to flatter me;
Just think if that hit me, it surely would scatter me.
I have ducked and I've dodged, but still they are after me;
They're the biggest, and I say 't ain't fair.
    I've heard you tell pa, too,
    A Frenchman's pure happiness
    Was a froggy's two hind legs
    Cooked up for a fancy dish.
    Now, if they get my legs,
    What good is there left of me,
    And how much for me would they care?
    Dip! Dodge! for there comes another!
    They just shied a dead cat,
    And it hit your big brother.
    See there like a big bomb-shell,
    It strikes in the marsh with a thud!
    Yes, child, and I'm thinking
    Of how we'll get out of this.
    Go this way. No, that way.

O, dear! how my legs twist!
Let's scream.
No!
Wring our hands, then.
I'll tell you what's better:
Let's settle way down in the mud.

All is now quiet; those boys are seeking other puddles, and the little community once more comes forth, but cautiously. Simon has returned, and is equipped for his journey.

The Prince calls his brothers about him, and tells them his plans, and seeks their aid.

I know a mousie fair,
   Who live in a quaint old mill,
Midst whirling sails and whistling gales,
   High up on a beautiful hill.
I've watched her oft at her spinning-wheel,
   But that she never knows.
I'd go and woo, but cannot walk
   With these corns upon my toes.

CHORUS.—   These corns upon my toes;
   The saddest of life's woes,
   Is trying to woo, to bill, and to coo,
   With corns upon the toes.

She has such silken ears,
   And, O, such silvery hair,
Her beautiful smellers are death to the fellers
   And drive me to despair.
Had I a steed, a fiery steed,
   Like a knight to meet his foes,
I'd sally forth,— but how could I mount,
   With these corns upon my toes?

This jewel in my head,
   I'd give for a noble steed,
No matter what, if legs he'd got,
   And a place to put these feet.
I'll ask my pollywog followers here,
   If they know any flunkey,
Of whom they think they might possibly steal
   A tolerably under-sized donkey.

   We know a donkey small,
   But you're so straight and tall,
   Your feet would touch.

   'T won't matter much.

   Well, then, he's just over that wall

Ah, ha! they've brought the noble steed —
'T is pity 't is no larger —
And now grasp thou the foaming bit,
While I bestride the charger.

They assist him to mount his humble steed, and see him safely on his way.

[END OF ACT FIRST.]

ACT SECOND.

Here we have the gypsy camp, for no modern opera would be complete without it. The gypsies are enjoying their camp life, and have evidently heard of the intended journey of the frog.

A frog he would a wooing go;
Heigho! said Rowly.
Whether his mother would let him or no,
With a rowly-powly, gammon and spinage;
Heigho! said Anthony Rowly.

Off he set, with his opera hat;
Heigho! said Rowly.
On the road he met with a rat,
With a rowly-powly, gammon and spinage;
Heigho! for Anthony Rowly!

They are rats in disguise as gypsies. The arrival of the Prince Frog and his retinue is a signal for a cessation of festivities, and they gather round the new comers.

They cure his corns in their own peculiar way, which seems effectual, though severe. This done, they go about their duties of camp life, apparently caring little for his presence, and singing their camp songs of

To-night, to-night, with wild delight,
The gypsy life we lead;
The fire's red light, the moonbeam bright,
And the dance upon the mead.
Oh, life has charms, but none so keen
As the forest joys we know;
The mountain stream, the firefly's gleam,
And mirth where'er we go.

Then, for the entertainment of the strangers, one of their number volunteers a song, in the chorus of which all join in certifying to their bravery.

GYPSY CAMP.   ACT II.

The life of a gypsy is jolly and free,
It seems in the opera like one steady spree;
Roaming the wide world o'er mountain and sea,
  With nothing to do but to steal.
Kidnapping babies from the highest of towers,
  Always getting the pink of them all;
Then jumping unscratched o'er a twenty-foot hedge,
  While the baby gives ne'er a squall.

CHO.—For we're gypsies so gay, light-fingered and fleet,
    As daring a band, too, as ever you'd meet,
    Telling fortunes to maidens and playing the sweet,
    Then like the mist passing away.

    We're opera gypsies, so pray don't suppose
      That one of the band ever paid for these clothes;
    But clothes-lines have suffered, and bonnets and bows,
      To rig up this vagabond crew.
    The wants of these fellows are boundless;
      Just now they are quite out of a job.
    But give them a chance. and they'll prig all your spoons,
      And pilfer the watch in your fob.

These gypsies have wonderful voices, of course,
They sleep on the damp ground but never get hoarse;
They travel in rain-storm, in snow-storm, and frost,
But never get stuffy or wheeze.
Their tempers are perfectly awful,
'Tis fearful to see them in rage;
It would scare you to death to meet them elsewhere,
But they're never seen off of the stage.

The wary old Baron Rat succeeds in getting the Prince Frog to tell his plan, but is surprised to find they so nearly affect his own interests. He calls abruptly for his wife, the Baroness, who also is present in disguise, to come forward and tell the fortune of the Prince, hoping by that means to frighten him from taking the journey. So Gypsy Meg (the assumed name of the Baroness) tries without success to turn him back.

Meg.—If you are seeking grandeur,
    Mistake not gilt for gold;
Snub fate, and then command her,
    Be watchful and be bold,
For fortune's fickle, though she smiles,
    And gracious seems to all.

Prince.—At fate I'll stare, nor heed it;
    On fortune I will frown;
Now take my hand and read it,
    Say naught to cast me down;
For 'neath this breast there beats a heart,
    That cannot, will not fail.

Meg.—O mortal man, take care! for see,
    Those lines are crossing here;
There's danger here before thee,
    And enemies are near,
Dark water here portends a death
    The bravest heart might fear.

[The following two verses are sung as duet.]

Prince.—I dare do all that man dare!
    The truth your looks betray:
For all your crew will pander,
    And truckle, too, for pay.
So farewell, Gypsy Meg, farewell
    Your arts are thrown away.

Meg.—Beware! for on that hand there
    A future is portrayed;
No courage can withstand her
    (Not such as you've displayed),
Beware! of gypsy's words there will
    Be proof ere close of day.

Having learned from the Rat that the two notorious villians, Sir Thomas Cat and Robber Kitten, are accustomed to follow the camp of the gypsies, the Prince and followers hide themselves to await their arrival.

The cats now appear, singing their own song of

> Hey, diddle, diddle, these cats and those fiddles,
>   The cow jumped over the moon,
> The little dog laughed to see so much sport,—ha, ha,
>   The dish ran away with the spoon.

A bargain is eventually made with these cats to do some villainous work, and Simon meets with some adventures, such as trying to fight a cow. He enters into the combat bravely, singing to keep up his courage.

COMBAT BETWEEN SIMPLE SIMON AND THE COW.

> I CAN be as big if I'm mind to,
>   As YOU, you great blundering fool;
> Ability's what you're blind to;
>   I've fought in a fencing school.
> Come, wake up, you wandering mooley cow,
>   I long for a tussle with thee:
> Now, here goes "one for his nobby,"
>   And here goes "two for his heels."
>
> If Simon is dead, now, we reckon,
>   The ladies all wish to inquire;
> We know that their dear hearts are waiting,
>   To welcome old Simon, the squire.
>   To welcome old Simon, the squire.
> We know that their dear hearts are waiting
>   To welcome old Simon, the squire.

DEPARTURE OF PRINCE FROG AND HIS RETAINERS.

After this they proceed on their journey to the mill.

The Queen arrives upon the scene too late; in fact, barely in time to see them as they vanish in the distance. She hoped to overtake him and turn him back. Her pollywogs are panting and breathless with the continued jumping they have been forced to keep up, and appeal in gasping tones for rest.

Oh, mother dear, now just look here,
  Now this will never do;
Oh pity our poor legs and feet,
  For don't you see they're new.
We never can keep up at all,
  If you go bouncing 'round;
We're like so many rubber balls
  That never cease to bound.
Oh, what's the cause of this hullabaloo,
  This everlasting row,
This hopping and kicking and jumping around,
  With no results to show.

The bewildered mother now breaks forth in anguish:—

Too late! too late! yes alas! too late!
Deluded child, this day will seal thy fate.
I cannot give thee o'er, I'll call thee back once more—
Froggie dear! hear! 'tis thy mother calls and bids thee wait for her;

I beseech thee! I implore thee! Oh, have pity on me.
He hears me not, or heeds me not.
Go! bring him back! Go! bring him back! my head! my brain!
Noble King! hear thy Queen while she implores thee,
Oh, guide our son, watch o'er our son, oh keep him from all harm;
Now thy spirit cheers me on, e'en while I call on thee,
Thy spirit bids me call once more, e'en while I call on thee,
I'll call once more! I'll call once more!
   Froggie dear! hear, etc.;
Now they seize him! now they bind him!
Now they hold him o'er the flames! now see them tear him!
Now see they're dancing! my brain is reeling! my boy! oh, my boy, Ah!
Froggie dear! hear! 'tis thy mother calls and bids thee wait for her.
I beseech thee! I implore thee! Oh have pity on me.
Mercy! — Mercy! — Mercy! — Mercy on me!

They having rested a little, try again the toilsome journey and disappear.

The cats, who have been quietly watching affairs and waiting opportunity, now come out from their hiding places and quarrel over the ill-gotten money.

> Miserable Kit, I suppose you're a-thinking
>   One-half this money belongs in your wallet.
> Miserable Cat, don't sit there a-blinking,
>   But remember you're a What-ye-may-call-it.
>
> Now there will be a row;
>   Now I will show you how;
> Who calls me liar, who calls me liar, will die!
>   Who's 'fraid of you? Who's 'fraid of you?
>
> Miserable Cat! your claws are now itching
>   To catch the same rat you pretend to admire.
> Miserable Cat! mine, too, are now stretching
>   To grapple your throat, for you call me a liar.
>
> This caterwauling squall
> Ends now in brawl;
> This caterwauling squall
> Ends now in brawl and mawl.

Fortunately the curtain falls upon this disgraceful strife.

[END OF ACT SECOND.]

ACT THIRD.

SCENE AT THE MILL. — Miss Mouse, our Martha, or our Marguerite, is discovered at the inevitable spinning-wheel of the opera.

She is the fair being who is to be wooed, and for whom all the preparations which we have seen, are made.

She is lonely, and thinks her lot a hard one, as it is—left an orphan by man's inhumanity to mice ; a generous uncle protects, while a very wicked aunt persecutes her.

She sees not the silver lining to her cloud, although, like the good little mouse she is, she tries to keep busy and cheerful.

The voice of the Prince Frog breaks forth in rapturous serenade, supported by the chorus of his stalwart followers, the pollywogs.

She is overwhelmed with joy, thinks it a dream, and joins in the chorus of welcome voices.

Soon the Prince enters and woos, in sweet song, the fair one, who replies in melody also — but mark the commendable obedience, under the circumstances, when she informs the ardent lover that she must first get the consent of her foster parent.

PRINCE FROG AND MISS MOUSE.

Prince. — " Star of my night! when shall we meet ?
When shall thy lips, love, sweet words repeat;
When shall our days peacefully glide ?
Never to part, love, come to my side.
Summer is waking, roses will bloom;
Shadows are breaking, dawn on my gloom,"
Dreaming of thee."

Chorus. — Dreaming of thee.   Bully for thee.
　　　　　Only of thee, still by thy side longing to be.

Prince. — Prithee, Miss Mouse are you within ?

Mouse. — O, yes, kind sir; and going to spin.

Prince. — Queen of my soul! when shall we meet ?
　　　　　O, let thy heart say come, I entreat.

Mouse. — Come, then, my lover, come I implore;
　　　　　Come with thy wooing; can I say more ?
　　　　　O! this, this for me ?   Is it a dream ?
　　　　　Will my bliss fly ? no, love never seems.

Prince and Chorus. —
　　　　　O, Mousie, for thee, only for thee!
　　　　　Still by thy side, love, longing to be.

Prince. — Prithee, Miss Mouse, marry to-night?
　　　　　I am a young frog, tall and upright.

Mouse. — My Uncle Rat went out this morn,
　　　　　I won't consent until his return.

Prince. — Here then I swear, love, by this fair hand,
　　　　　Thee I will marry, if I can.

Mouse. — This, this for me, etc.

Chorus. — Mousie, for thee, etc.

Her brightest dreams are realized when she finds the rank and position of her lover to be that of a prince.

The course of true love is not allowed to run smooth; it would not be correct to do so, hence we have The Crafty Aunt, the sudden announcement of important business, which calls the lover back to camp, Miss Mousie's anxiety as to the final decision of her uncle, and her apparent success in winning her aunt's favor to the lover and his suit.

　　　　　O, Aunty dear, now don't you know ?
　　　　　Your heart in flutters used to go
　　　　　At the thought of Uncle Rat.

　　　　　O, yes, my child; but don't you see ?
　　　　　This frog is not so fair to me
　　　　　As a fine full-whiskered rat!

　　　　　O, Aunty dear, now don't you see ?
　　　　　This froggy looks as bright to me
　　　　　As a mouse or whiskered rat.

　　　　　I see, my child; it is no use,
　　　　　You've got your head in a pretty noose;
　　　　　You have, and that's a fact.

And now, my child, let's live in peace.
Your uncle's anger I'll appease
With all a woman's wile.

Now, Aunty dear, my troth I'll plight,
And have the wedding here to-night,
In this same dear old mill.

Baron Rat arrives, and with the usual keen sense of rats, discovers
that a stranger has been there, and in answer to their inquiries, replies—

Call it not fancy, say 'tis not fear,
When senses like mine tell me some one's been here.
No craft or no cunning that ever was seen
Can compass my wits or scent quick and keen;
There is odor of marsh, there is flavor of fern,
There are footprints of strangers wherever I turn.
I am sharp to discern, of my wrath you I warn;
Now tell me who's been here since I have been gone;
Now tell me who's been here since I have been gone.
    Do not deceive me, do not deceive me,
    My watchful spirit is guarding you still.

Dutiful Mousie, bless your dear heart,
Your uncle is paid by your candor in part;
But gay serenaders loitering here,
Betoken that Cupid is hovering near.

    O, beware of your head, O, beware of your heart,
For often when love comes the reason departs.
I have seen many years, so dear Mousie, believe
That I will protect you if you'll not deceive;
That I will protect you if you'll not deceive.

His consent is gained.   Mousie is made happy by being sent to invite
the Prince and all his followers to the wedding.

It now appears that while Mrs. Rat is plotting the destruction of Miss
Mouse, Mr. Rat hopes to destroy the frog, never suspecting the treachery of the two cats.

Baroness. — Not the wedding, or this dressing,
        Bring me half the care
    As the awful task perplexing,
        Dressing my back hair !
    Shall I braid or shall I twist it ?
        Loop, or knot, or bow ?
    Twice alike I dare not wear it, —
        That were death I know.
    If Mrs. Grundy saw me,
        Though my best I try,
    She would say, while she abhorred me,
        Is not she a guy ?

2

I should die, I know t'would kill me
  To be thought a guy.
A guy ? not I ! a guy ? not I !

World and fashion keep me worried ;
  Be I ne'er so fair,
They will laugh and say, how horrid
  She does her back hair ;
Fuzz, or frizz, or plait, or kink it,
  Fashion's eyes are keen ;
I 'm condemned before I think it,
  When my hair is seen.
Unless the last new wrinkle
  Of some queenly crown
Waves behind in truthful crinkle,
  I am frowned upon.
Though I die, I 'll have that wrinkle,
  If I fuss till morn !
A guy ? not I ! a guy ? not I !

During the absence of every one, the cats enter to look over the field
of their coming treachery and lay their plans.

Kit. —
I 'll sing a mournful ditty of pussy in a well ;
J. Green he was the miscreant by which the act befel ;
Her life was saved in ample time ; J. Stout, as he passed by,
Jerked pussy from a sloppy grave, and then cracked J. Green's eye.

They saw how wet poor pussy was, and sent for great J. Stout,
Who set the bells to ringing for to have the cat wrung out,
And puss got soon so she sot up, and fixed her fuzzy fur;
And J. Green, humbly passing by, he asked her how she were.

That same old cat is living now, though every hair is gray,
Her tail is crooked, her eyes are dim, but still she purrs away.
J. Green is poor; he begs his bread, each day he draws his breath;
J. Stout is now a nobleman, and will be till his death.

Chorus. — Ding dong bell, pussy's in the well;
    Who put her in ? Why little Johnny Green you know.
    Who pulled her out ? Why, great John Stout.
    Now that was rough on pussy.

Tom. — At the door I 'll stand, while you rush in,
    And slaughter whom you may.
    Crack the old rat's crown, pull the old wife down ;
    And then we 'll run away.

Kit. — O, yes ! I see ; I 'll do all the work,
    While you no danger share ;
    I hate above all the world a shirk,
    Who dares not tumble his hair.

You are a shirk and a sneaking cat,
I 'll tangle my claws in your hair.

Tom. — I 'm not a shirk — and for calling me that
Look out for your eyes and hair.

Chorus. — More rows ! more rows ! hurrah for more rows !
We 'll carouse, till we arouse more rows.

Kit. — A better plan comes in my head,
I 'll tell you what we 'll do.
Like two vile ghosts, we 'll frighten the hosts,
Then I 'LL devour the two.

Tom. — That's you, clear through; you leave me none,
But take the lion's share;
Now can 't you afford to leave me a bone,
Or may be the hide and hair ?
I vow to you there never was known
So corrupt a cantankerous cat.

Kit. — I bow to your lordship ; there is just one
Who can teach me for all that.

Chorus. — More rows, more rows, etc.

Kit. — Whose row is this ? I should like to know !

Tom. — 'Tis yours ! for you sauced me first.

Kit. — Just say that again and I 'll give you a pain.

Tom. — Try it now and see who 'll get the worst.

Kit (scared). —
O fudge ! such friends as you and I
Should never bickering be.

Tom. — That's so, my son, I was only in fun.
Such folly I never did see.

Both. — O, what a poor row we had just now !
O, what a poor row ! poor row !
Of all the poor rows, that row just now
Is the poorest that I know.

Chorus. — Of all the poor rows, that row, etc.

They disappear, and the scene changes to a wood near the mill, when
Simon enters melancholy and cast down, and sings about his dreaded
foe, the cow.

In me you may behold
A sorry frog, ex-pollywog,
Grim-visaged, stern, and bold,
With terror almost numb.

Tho' looking ferocious, I have an atrocious
Desire to run. I can't see the fun
Appearing heroic. A coward—I know it—
And can't help but show it,
Or fright overcome.
Oh, why — did I — as squire — ere apply ?
Oh! what a silly frog, to leave my bog
And mossy log,— quiet brook, — shady nook,
    And stump.
My Pollywoggy paradise,—
Squirming worms, — buzzing flies, —
Crawling gnats, — tittle bàts —
    Oh! Kerchunk!
Oh, what a silly frog, etc., etc.

A reputation gained
    For bravery. What slavery
The laurels to maintain,
When I shiver, and quake, and shake;
If I had some strychnine I'd poison that bovine.
Some friendly stone wall, quick through it I'd crawl.
I'm all in a tremor,
This two-horned dilemma,
No way, shape or manner,
    Can I escape.
I vow — that cow — will now — row — anyhow,
Oh! what a silly frog, to leave my bog,
And mossy log, etc., etc., etc.

At close of Simon's song the frogs and pollywogs, having made
friends with the rats, enter arm in arm. Simon joins them, and leads
the procession to the wedding at the mill. The scene is once more
changed, and the old mill is discovered, where all is joy and mirth.

Now let the old mill ring,
    Hip, hip, hurrah!
Now let us drink and sing,
    Hip, hip, hurrah!
Drink to the Prince and bride so gay!
All hail this happy wedding-day!
When bride and queen we take in joy away,
    Hip, hip, hurrah!

Come fill your glasses up;
    Hip, hip, hurrah!
Come quaff the flowing cup;
    Hip, hip, hurrah!
Health to our noble baroness!
Health, wealth, and the purest happiness!
Let glasses clink now as we pledge the rest —
    Hip, hip, hurrah!

The Prince is called upon for a song, but he, too, is anxious for the cats to arrive, and begs Miss Mouse to sing instead.

> I sit and spin this summer day,
> My heart in dream-land far away.
> Sadly I sing, no one to love,
> No loving heart to cheer me.
> With busy wheel I strive to still
> The ceaseless droning of the mill;
> The summer breeze blows soft and warm,
> But brings no lovers here.
> What do I hear? 'T is a song from the skies.
> 'T is but thy fancy, my faint heart replies.
> Star of my night, sang a voice full and free,
> Still, by thy side, love, longing to be.
> Then I sang gay, with merry heart,
> Oh, come and woo, with lover's art.
> Brightly he came, like morn's first rays,
> My restless heart to still.

THE FLIGHT OF PRINCE FROG.

> Future, bright future, seems so near,
> With all its wealth of promise here,
> And fills my life with heavenly dreams
> Of blissful, happy days.

Lonely no more, at thy dear side,
Thou wilt protect thy loving bride.
To-morrow we will wend our way
To thy ancestral halls.
I shall be queen, there, of all I survey,
With vassals and serfs at my feet all the day.
Visions of bliss, wilt thou shine evermore?
Oh, leave me not yet to the sadness of yore!
Then I sing gay, with merry heart,
For thou, my Prince, my lover art;
My brightest dreams thou hast fulfilled;
My restless heart is still.

The cats now come rushing in, do their murderous work, and look on.

The frog, seeing all, and fearing for his own life, bids all good-night in a most cowardly manner, and leaves the scene. He is soon discovered by Miss Mousie, struggling fearfully for his life in mortal combat with a lily-white duck.

All try to cheer him with song, and all are confident that the valor of their Prince will yet save him; but alas! it was an unusually smart duck.

O, he will win! O, he will win!
O, he will win who loves a mouse so fair!
Knows how to win, knows how to win,
Knows how to win, who loves a mouse so fair.
So here's an end of one, two, three, —
The rat, the mouse, and the little froggy!

Lightning Source UK Ltd.
Milton Keynes UK
UKHW050823130522
402874UK00025B/5